Preface

Begum Rokeya was among the most prominent Bengali Muslim feminists of the early twentieth century. At sixteen, she married the much older Deputy Magistrate of Bhagalpur. As an elite Bengali Muslim woman, she did not go to school and lived strict purdah (a religious and social practice of secluding women and girls from non-kin men). With the support of her brother who was undertaking a British style education, Begum Rokeya cultivated her own education at home. Her husband died young and with the money left to her she opened the first school for Muslim girls in Calcutta, which still exists today. A prominent social reformer, she also founded the Calcutta chapter of the Anjuman-i-Khawatin-i-Islam, the primary women's organization for Muslim women in India. Writing in Bengali as well as English, she penned numerous essays toward instigating the "awakening" of Muslim women. She harshly condemned women's restricted lives in purdah, as well as claims of their spiritual and biological inferiority. In the portrait gallery of Dhaka's Pink Palace museum, Begum Rokeya is the single female face dignifying the walls.

Begum Rokeya published "Sultana's Dream" as a short English-language story in *The Indian Ladies Magazine*, a publication for "modern" Indian women. The story is narrated by an elite woman protagonist from her luxurious secluded chambers. The protagonist falls asleep as she is "thinking lazily of the condition of Indian womanhood."

She then wakes into a dream.

Alert within her imaginary, she finds herself walking unveiled in daylight in another world where the gendered structures of Indian Muslim society are reversed: men are now confined to mardana (the name of the outer part of a household for men and guests, in complement to zenana, the inner part of a household reserved for women). In this world turned upside down, women are unveiled in public, acting as the rulers and scientists of this alternative way of being. "Lady" scientists have turned away from building military machines and instead invent ways to harness rain from the sky and share energy from the sun. One school of women scientists "invented a wonderful balloon, to which they attached a number of pipes. By means of this captive balloon which they managed to keep afloat above the cloud-land, they could draw as much water from the atmosphere as they pleased." Another university "invented an instrument by which they could collect as much sun-heat as they wanted. And they kept the heat stored up to be distributed among others as required."

Relishing her new public freedom, the protagonist learns the history behind this fantastical otherworld. Not long ago, these scientific feats were dismissed by the male-dominated military society as "sentimental nightmares." The revolution in gender roles, and the celebration of the women's science, had been achieved by a violent military victory. The male-run military had failed to repel an invasion by another country resulting in the tremendous loss of life. In a final bid to resist the invasion, the exhausted men agreed to retire to seclusion at their homes and turn the war over to the women. Female scientists then unleashed their sun-heat on the enemy, burning them down, and winning dominion over their country. Through this act of mass violence, a new society, and scientific culture, was born.

The most distinguished science of this dream world was botany. The roads were formed of a "soft carpet" of moss and flowers, and the city itself was a marvelous garden.

Sewing, too, was a celebrated art, and beauty highly valued. In the garden, "[e]very creeper, every tomato plant was itself an ornament," such that the products of science were as much aesthetic as functional, and science itself was not divorced from feelings.

"Sentimental" science, saturated with feeling and kinship, was esteemed. This rearrangement of sentiment extended to society itself. Here, all women were educated, and married late, while men minded the children. Kinship was expanded such that "a distant cousin is as sacred as a brother."

Thriving in a city built out of the botanical and ecological feats of science, science itself expressed new kinds of affective relations. In the end, the narrator abruptly falls out of the dream to find herself back in her lounge chair, which was also back in her own zenana.

Penned in a "real world" zenana, "Sultana's Dream" summons an early twentieth century feminist technoscience through a counterfactual world, a world turned inside out. Awake to its projections, the story invites oppressed women to dream *with* technoscience, social-relations, and nature at a moment of agitation for access to formal education and South Asian feminism. Yet, the story does not reverse all axes of inequality. "Ladyland" is ruled by a Queen and the narrative leaves aristocracy and class hierarchy in place as a benevolent form of rule. While the inversion of men's and women's worlds reverses, rather than unravels, binary gendered norms and compulsory heterosexuality, the text influentially summons into apprehension the radical potential of another way of doing technoscience, and the very possibility of contesting the naturalization of the present. Begum Rokeya would herself become one of the most revered women in the history of Bangladesh, and "Sultana's Dream" would become a celebrated inspiration for a different world right into the present.

Written in a place and century when agricultural practices were being rearranged by colonial regimes and capitalism, "Sultana's Dream" elevated botany, one of the few sciences gendered feminine and open to amateur women, as the pivot for an alternative form of expert rule. In this way, the story can be read as containing a decolonizing politics: offering an uncolonized otherwise in which science becomes non-violent, sustains life, and is endemic to women and South Asian culture. In conjuring a phantasma of ecological, plant-centric science, Sultana's Dream presages the emergence of strong environmental and ecological feminisms in South Asia, from the Chipko movement to the internationally known ecofeminism of Vandana Shiva, or the ecological farming movement of Nayakrishi Andolon and the seed sharing work of UBINIG. Through its figures of gardens, clouds and pleasure, "Sultana's Dream" suggests the possibility that subjects who dream with technoscience might do life, gender, kinship, and nation differently.

One important way of reading this story is to celebrate the authorship of an eminent Bengali Muslim woman writer, feminist, and social reformer in the early twentieth century. Adding to this recognition, the text might also be read as an invitation to think about the relationship between technoscience, futurity, gender, and dreaming. Sultana's Dream can be situated along a genre of Western utopian writing that used the trope of the dream as the entrance into conjuring another world.

More than this, in colonial Bengal, dreaming was charged with other histories and forces. Dreams hold a special role in Islamic history and in The Qu'ran.

The Prophet Muhammed's revelations included dreams that were divinely inspired. Dream interpretation was an established feature of medieval Muslim literature and practice, and a thick history of dream interpretation exists in Bengal.

Dreams can have a prophetic potential, and offer divinely inspired insights and valued knowledge. Such dream-visions can happen both when asleep and awake, as waking visions. Importantly, they are understood to come to the dreamer as opposed to being produced or authored by her. In the book *Dreams that Matter,* about "dreaming in the undreamy time" of recent Egypt, anthropologist Amira Mittermaier traces the history of Islamic dream interpretation, warning against the all too frequent temptation of Western scholarship to want to interpret the "unconscious" meaning of dreams, and assign dreams to subjects. Mittermaier instead situates Islamic dream interpretation in a long history of Islamic philosophical and theological contemplation that ponders the difficulty of distinguishing between wakefulness and dream, or between our thinking and reality.

The historian Projit Mukharji, writing about colonial Bengal, draws out the importance of dreamscapes as potent intangibles within South Asian traditional medical practices.

Dreams, he has argued, were a well of divine inspiration for innovative new treatments. Dreams had epistemic authority that conferred divine force onto new remedies or practices. Thus, dreams are not mere flights of fancy or creations of the unconscious. They are a source of world-making that are interacted with and bring potential, insight and innovation into the world. Dreaming can be the perception of an intangible presence or potential in a world saturated with intangibilities and held together by imaginaries. The recognition of the powerful world making capacities of nonsecular dreaming in Islamic and Bengali dream practice, pushes back on Benjamin's analysis of phantasmagoria to underline that technoscience is as just one of many modalities of wakeful dreaming. Technoscientific speculation, joins an already rich array of potent practices that apprehend the immaterial and felt as a historical force.

Read through this history of potent dreaming, "Sultana's Dream" hails women and girls as aspirational and generative subjects of technoscience and as crucial to the constitution of an anticipatory postcolonial nation. Women become the agents and not just the objects of speculation. Begum Rokeya described her social reform work as part of an "awakening" of women. Sultana's Dream "awakens" readers to an alternate possibility, even though the narrator herself concludes by waking back into the complexity of her luxurious oppression. Feminist technoscience is affirmatively performed in the dream, and more than this, Sultana's Dream summons other futures through the speculative potential of technoscience. Today, the story is still active as an inspiration towards fashioning a future otherwise, a stimulus to art exhibits and inspiring contemporary feminist ecological practices. The text offers dreaming as a generative force that can affectively and politically reorient the potentials in the world. In its narrative construction, the story is very much awake to the force of that dreaming. It is a speculative imaginary that works to unfix its 1905 present and summon other futures, even if improbable, for both women and science.

What would it mean to be awake to the dream, to become alert to the varieties of imaginative force and feeling that make up technoscience? I want to take seriously the suggestion that technoscience is potent for its ability to create not only facts, but also affectively charged temporized imaginaries. Can one say that a characteristic of technoscience is that it induces dreamscapes, in this instance, nonsubjective imaginaries conjured by the practices of colonial science, by the numbers of development indexes, by the tickertape of stock markets, by the graphs of demography? What does it look like to let go of the author function in our histories of speculation and speculative fiction, and instead attend, like Benjamin, to the collective phantasma that accompany the built and inhabited world?

In this way, Begum Rokeya did not just author "Sultana's Dream" about technoscience, it was at least partly animated by the rise of speculation about girls and women that technoscience (then colonial, now postcolonial) helped to create. The story dreams *with and through* (not just about) technoscience.

Thus, we might see the speculative futurity in "Sultana's Dream" as doing more than subverting the figure of woman within the colonial goalposts of modernity and tradition. "Sultana's Dream," perhaps, participates affirmatively in a technoscientific project that figured women and girls as contested postcolonial speculative subjects. It signals the emergence of affectively charged speculative temporization through which feminism, postcolonialism, development, capitalism, and nationalism would all come to operate in the dreamscape of the twentieth century.

********

# Sultana's Dream

One evening I was lounging in an easy chair in my bedroom and thinking lazily of the condition of Indian womanhood. I am not sure whether I dozed off or not. But, as far as I remember, I was wide awake. I saw the moonlit sky sparkling with thousands of diamond-like stars, very distinctly.

All on a sudden a lady stood before me; how she came in, I do not know. I took her for my friend, Sister Sara.

"Good morning," said Sister Sara. I smiled inwardly as I knew it was not morning, but starry night. However, I replied to her, saying, "How do you do?"

"I am all right, thank you. Will you please come out and have a look at our garden?"

I looked again at the moon through the open window, and thought there was no harm in going out at that time. The men-servants outside were fast asleep just then, and I could have a pleasant walk with Sister Sara.

I used to have my walks with Sister Sara, when we were at Darjeeling. Many a time did we walk hand in hand and talk light-heartedly in the botanical gardens there. I fancied, Sister Sara had probably come to take me to some such garden and I readily accepted her offer and went out with her.

When walking I found to my surprise that it was a fine morning. The town was fully awake and the streets alive with bustling crowds. I was feeling very shy, thinking I was walking in the street in broad daylight, but there was not a single man visible.

Some of the passers-by made jokes at me. Though I could not understand their language, yet I felt sure they were joking. I asked my friend, "What do they say?"

"The women say that you look very mannish."

"Mannish?" said I, "What do they mean by that?"

"They mean that you are shy and timid like men."

"Shy and timid like men?" It was really a joke. I became very nervous, when I found that my companion was not Sister Sara, but a stranger. Oh, what a fool had I been to mistake this lady for my dear old friend, Sister Sara.

She felt my fingers tremble in her hand, as we were walking hand in hand.

"What is the matter, dear?" she said affectionately. "I feel somewhat awkward," I said in a rather apologizing tone, "as being a purdahnishin woman I am not accustomed to walking abut unveiled."

"You need not be afraid of coming across a man here. This is Ladyland, free from sin and harm. Virtue herself reigns here."

By and by I was enjoying the scenery. Really it was very grand. I mistook a patch of green grass for a velvet cushion. Feeling as if I were walking on a soft carpet, I looked down and found the path covered with moss and flowers.

"How nice it is," said I.

"Do you like it?" asked Sister Sara. (I continued calling her "Sister Sara," and she kept calling me by my name).

"Yes, very much; but I do not like to tread on the tender and sweet flowers."

"Never mind, dear Sultana; your treading will not harm them; they are street flowers."

"The whole place looks like a garden," said I admiringly. "You have arranged every plant so skillfully."

"Your Calcutta could become a nicer garden than this if only your countrymen wanted to make it so."

"They would think it useless to give so much attention to horticulture, while they have so many other things to do."

"They could not find a better excuse," said she with smile.

I became very curious to know where the men were. I met more than a hundred women while walking there, but not a single man.

"Where are the men?" I asked her.

"In their proper places, where they ought to be."

"Pray let me know what you mean by 'their proper places'."

"O, I see my mistake, you cannot know our customs, as you were never here before. We shut our men indoors."

"Just as we are kept in the zenana?"

"Exactly so."

"How funny," I burst into a laugh. Sister Sara laughed too.

"But dear Sultana, how unfair it is to shut in the harmless women and let loose the men."

"Why? It is not safe for us to come out of the zenana, as we are naturally weak."

"Yes, it is not safe so long as there are men about the streets, nor is it so when a wild animal enters a marketplace."

"Of course not."

"Suppose, some lunatics escape from the asylum and begin to do all sorts of mischief to men, horses and other creatures; in that case what will your countrymen do?"

"They will try to capture them and put them back into their asylum."

"Thank you! And you do not think it wise to keep sane people inside an asylum and let loose the insane?"

"Of course not!" said I laughing lightly.

"As a matter of fact, in your country this very thing is done! Men, who do or at least are capable of doing no end of mischief, are let loose and the innocent women, shut up in the zenana! How can you trust those untrained men out of doors?"

"We have no hand or voice in the management of our social affairs. In India man is lord and master, he has taken to himself all powers and privileges and shut up the women in the zenana."

"Why do you allow yourselves to be shut up?"

"Because it cannot be helped as they as stronger than women."

"A lion is stronger than a man, but it does not enable him to dominate the human race. You have neglected the duty you owe to yourselves and you have lost your natural rights by shutting your eyes to your own interests."

"But my dear sister Sara, if we do everything by ourselves, what will the men do then?"

"They should not do anything, excuse me; they are fit for nothing. Only catch them and put them into the zenana."

"But would it be very easy to catch and put them inside the four walls?" said I. "And even if this were done, would all their business, political and commercial - also go with them into the zenana?"

Sister Sara made no reply. She only smiled sweetly. Perhaps she thought it useless to argue with one who was no better than a frog in a well.

By this time we reached sister Sara's house. It was situated in a beautiful heart-shaped garden. It was a bungalow with a corrugated iron roof. It was cooler and nicer than any of our rich buildings. I cannot describe how neat and how nicely furnished and how tastefully decorated it was.

We sat side by side. She brought out of the parlour a piece of embroidery work and began putting on a fresh design.

"Do you know knitting and needle work?"

"Yes; we have nothing else to do in our zenana."

"But we do not trust our zenana members with embroidery!" she said laughing, "as a man has not patience enough to pass thread through a needle hole even!"

"Have you done all this work yourself?" I asked her pointing to the various pieces of embroidered teapoy cloths.

"Yes."

"How can you find time to do all these? You have to do the office work as well? Have you not?"

"Yes. I do not stick to the laboratory all day long. I finish my work in two hours."

"In two hours! How do you manage? In our land the officers, magistrates -- for instance, work seven hours daily."

"I have seen some of them doing their work. Do you think they work all the seven hours?"

"Certainly they do!"

"No, dear Sultana, they do not. They dawdle away their time in smoking. Some smoke two or three choroots during the office time. They talk much about their work, but do little. Suppose one choroot takes half an hour to burn off, and a man smokes twelve choroots daily; then you see, he wastes six hours every day in sheer smoking."

We talked on various subjects, and I learned that they were not subject to any kind of epidemic disease, nor did they suffer from mosquito bites as we do. I was very much astonished to hear that in Ladyland no one died in youth except by rare accident.

"Will you care to see our kitchen?" she asked me.

"With pleasure," said I, and we went to see it. Of course the men had been asked to clear off when I was going there. The kitchen was situated in a beautiful vegetable garden. Every creeper, every tomato plant was itself an ornament. I found no smoke, nor any chimney either in the kitchen -- it was clean and bright; the windows were decorated with flower gardens. There was no sign of coal or fire.

"How do you cook?" I asked.

"With solar heat," she said, at the same time showing me the pipe, through which passed the concentrated sunlight and heat. And she cooked something then and there to show me the process.

"How did you manage to gather and store up the sun heat?" I asked her in amazement.

"Let me tell you a little of our past history then. Thirty years ago, when our present Queen was thirteen years old, she inherited the throne. She was Queen in name only, the Prime Minister really ruling the country.

"Our good Queen liked science very much. She circulated an order that all the women in her country should be educated. Accordingly a number of girls' schools were founded and supported by the government . Education was spread far and wide among women. And early marriage also was stopped. No woman was to be allowed to marry before she was twenty-one. I must tell you that, before this change we had been kept in strict purdah."

"How the tables are turned," I interposed with a laugh.

"But the seclusion is the same," she said. "In a few years we had separate universities, where no men were admitted."

"In the capital, where our Queen lives, there are two universities. One of these invented a wonderful balloon, to which they attached a number of pipes.

By means of this captive balloon which they managed to keep afloat above the cloud-land, they could draw as much water from the atmosphere as they pleased. As the water was incessantly being drawn by the university people no cloud gathered and the ingenious Lady Principal stopped rain and storms thereby."

"Really! Now I understand why there is no mud here!" said I. But I could not understand how it was possible to accumulate water in the pipes. She explained to me how it was done, but I was unable to understand her, as my scientific knowledge was very limited. However, she went on...

"When the other university came to know of this, they became exceedingly jealous and tried to do something more extraordinary still. They invented an instrument by which they could collect as much sun-heat as they wanted. And they kept the heat stored up to be distributed among others as required.

"While the women were engaged in scientific research, the men of this country were busy increasing their military power. When they came to know that the female universities were able to draw water from the atmosphere and collect heat from the sun, they only laughed at the members of the universities and called the whole thing 'a sentimental nightmare'!"

"Your achievements are very wonderful indeed! But tell me, how you managed to put the men of your country into the zenana. Did you entrap them first?"

"No."

"It is not likely that they would surrender their free and open air life of their own accord and confine themselves within the four walls of the zenana! They must have been overpowered."

"Yes, they have been!"

"By whom? By some lady warriors, I suppose?"

"No, not by arms."

"Yes, it cannot be so. Men's arms are stronger than women's. Then?"

"By brain."

"Even their brains are bigger and heavier than women's. Are they not?"

"Yes, but what of that? An elephant also has got a bigger and heavier brain than a man has. Yet man can enchain elephants and employ them, according to their own wishes."

"Well said, but tell me please, how it all actually happened. I am dying to know it!"

"Women's brains are somewhat quicker than men's. Ten years ago, when the military officers called our scientific discoveries 'a sentimental nightmare,' some of the young ladies wanted to say something in reply to those remarks. But both the Lady Principals restrained them and said, they should reply not by word, but by deed, if ever they got the opportunity. And they had not long to wait for that opportunity."

"How marvelous!" I heartily clapped my hands. "And now the proud gentlemen are dreaming sentimental dreams themselves."

"Soon afterwards certain persons came from a neighbouring country and took shelter in ours. They were in trouble having committed some political offense. The king who cared more for power than for good government asked our kind-hearted Queen to hand them over to his officers. She refused, as it was against her principle to turn out refugees. For this refusal the king declared war against our country.

"Our military officers sprang to their feet at once and marched out to meet the enemy.

"The enemy however, was too strong for them. Our soldiers fought bravely, no doubt. But in spite of all their bravery the foreign army advanced step by step to invade our country."

"Nearly all the men had gone out to fight; even a boy of sixteen was not left home. Most of our warriors were killed, the rest driven back and the enemy came within twenty-five miles of the capital.

"A meeting of a number of wise ladies was held at the Queen's palace to advise as to what should be done to save the land.

"Some proposed to fight like soldiers; others objected and said that women not trained to fight with swords and guns, nor were they accustomed to fighting with any weapons. A third party regretfully remarked that they were hopelessly weak of body.

"'If you cannot save your country for lack of physical strength,' said the Queen, 'try to do so by brain power.'

"There was a dead silence for a few minutes. Her Royal Highness said again, 'I must commit suicide if the land and my honour are lost.'

"Then the Lady Principal of the second university (who had collected sun-heat), who had been silently thinking during the consultation, remarked that they were all but lost, and there was little hope left for them. There was, owever, one plan which she would like to try, and this would be her first and ast efforts; if she failed in this, there would be nothing left but to commit uicide. All present solemnly vowed that they would never allow themselves to e enslaved, on matter what happened.

"The Queen thanked them heartily, and asked the Lady Principal to try her lan.

"The Lady Principal rose again and said, 'before we go out the men must nter the zenanas. I make this prayer for the sake of purdah.' 'Yes, of course,' eplied Her Royal Highness.

"On the following day the Queen called upon all men to retire into zenanas or the sake of honour and liberty.

"Wounded and tired as they were, they took that order rather for a boon! 'hey bowed low and entered the zenanas without uttering a single word of rotest. They were sure that there was no hope for this country at all.

"Then the Lady Principal with her two thousand students marched to the attle field, and arriving there directed all the rays of the concentrated sunlight nd heat towards the enemy.

"The heat and light were too much for them to bear. They all ran away anic-stricken, not knowing in their bewilderment how to counteract that scorching heat. When they fled away leaving their guns and other ammunitions of war, they were burnt down by means of the same sun heat.

"Since then no one has tried to invade our country any more."

"And since then your countrymen never tried to come out of the zenana?"

"Yes, they wanted to be free. Some of the police commissioners and district magistrates sent word to the Queen to the effect that the military officers certainly deserved to be imprisoned for their failure; but they never neglected their duty and therefore they should not be punished and they prayed to be restored to their respective offices.

"Her Royal Highness sent them a circular letter intimating to them that if their services should ever be needed they would be sent for, and that in the meanwhile they should remain where they were.

"Now that they are accustomed to the purdah system and have ceased to grumble at their seclusion, we call the system 'Murdana' instead of 'zenana'."

"But how do you manage," I asked Sister Sara, "to do without the police or magistrates in case of theft or murder?"

"Since the 'Murdana' system has been established, there has been no more crime or sin; therefore we do not require a policeman to find out a culprit, nor do we want a magistrate to try a criminal case."

"That is very good, indeed. I suppose if there was any dishonest person, you could very easily chastise her. As you gained a decisive victory without shedding a single drop of blood, you could drive off crime and criminals too without much difficulty!"

"Now, dear Sultana, will you sit here or come to my parlour?" she asked me.

"Your kitchen is not inferior to a queen's boudoir!" I replied with a pleasant smile, "but we must leave it now; for the gentlemen may be cursing me for keeping them away from their duties in the kitchen so long." We both laughed heartily.

"How my friends at home will be amused and amazed, when I go back and tell them that in the far-off Ladyland, ladies rule over the country and control all social matters, while gentlemen are kept in the Murdanas to mind babies, to cook and to do all sorts of domestic work; and that cooking is so easy a thing that it is simply a pleasure to cook!"

"Yes, tell them about all that you see here."

"Please let me know, how you carry on land cultivation and how you plough the land and do other hard manual work."

"Our fields are tilled by means of electricity, which supplies motive power for other hard work as well, and we employ it for our aerial conveyances too. We have no rail road nor any paved streets here."

"Therefore neither street nor railway accidents occur here," said I. "Do not you ever suffer from want of rainwater?" I asked.

"Never since the 'water balloon' has been set up. You see the big balloon and pipes attached thereto. By their aid we can draw as much rainwater as we require. Nor do we ever suffer from flood or thunderstorms. We are all very busy making nature yield as much as she can. We do not find time to quarrel with one another as we never sit idle. Our noble Queen is exceedingly fond of botany; it is her ambition to convert the whole country into one grand garden."

"The idea is excellent. What is your chief food?"

"Fruits."

"How do you keep your country cool in hot weather? We regard the rainfall in summer as a blessing from heaven."

"When the heat becomes unbearable, we sprinkle the ground with plentiful showers drawn from the artificial fountains. And in cold weather we keep our room warm with sun heat."

She showed me her bathroom, the roof of which was removable. She could enjoy a shower bath whenever she liked, by simply removing the roof (which was like the lid of a box) and turning on the tap of the shower pipe.

"You are a lucky people!" ejaculated I. "You know no want. What is you religion, may I ask?"

"Our religion is based on Love and Truth. It is our religious duty to love one another and to be absolutely truthful. If any person lies, she or he is...."

"Punished with death?"

"No, not with death. We do not take pleasure in killing a creature of God, especially a human being. The liar is asked to leave this land for good and never to come to it again."

"Is an offender never forgiven?"

"Yes, if that person repents sincerely."

"Are you not allowed to see any man, except your own relations?"

"No one except sacred relations."

"Our circle of sacred relations is very limited; even first cousins are not sacred."

"But ours is very large; a distant cousin is as sacred as a brother."

"That is very good. I see purity itself reigns over your land. I should like to see the good Queen, who is so sagacious and far-sighted and who has made all these rules."

"All right," said Sister Sara.

Then she screwed a couple of seats onto a square piece of plank. To this plank she attached two smooth and well-polished balls. When I asked her what the balls were for, she said they were hydrogen balls and they were used to overcome the force of gravity. The balls were of different capacities to be used according to the different weights desired to be overcome. She then fastened to the air-car two wing-like blades, which, she said, were worked by electricity. After we were comfortably seated she touched a knob and the blades began to whirl, moving faster and faster every moment. At first we were raised to the height of about six or seven feet and then off we flew. And before I could realize that we had commenced moving, we reached the garden of the Queen.

My friend lowered the air-car by reversing the action of the machine, and when the car touched the ground the machine was stopped and we got out.

I had seen from the air-car the Queen walking on a garden path with her little daughter (who was four years old) and her maids of honour.

"Halloo! You here!" cried the Queen addressing Sister Sara. I was introduced to Her Royal Highness and was received by her cordially without any ceremony.

I was very much delighted to make her acquaintance. In the course of the conversation I had with her, the Queen told me that she had no objection to permitting her subjects to trade with other countries. "But," she continued, no trade was possible with countries where the women were kept in the zenanas and so unable to come and trade with us. Men, we find, are rather of lower morals and so we do not like dealing with them. We do not covet other people's land, we do not fight for piece of diamond though it may be a thousand-fold brighter than the Koh-i-Noor, nor do we grudge a ruler his peacock throne. We dive deep into the ocean of knowledge and try to find out the precious gems, which Nature has kept in store for us. We enjoy Nature's gifts as much as we can."

After taking leave of the Queen, I visited the famous universities, and was shown some of their manufactories, laboratories and observatories.

After visiting the above places of interest we got again into the air-car, but as soon as it began moving, I somehow slipped down and the fall startled me out of my dream. And on opening my eyes, I found myself in my own bed

lounging in the easy-chair!